The 3-D Library of the Human Body

THE EYE
LEARNING HOW WE SEE

Jennifer Viegas

Editor's Note

The idea for the illustrations in this book originated in 1986 with the Vesalius Project at Colorado State University's Department of Anatomy and Neurobiology. There, a team of scientists and illustrators dreamed of turning conventional two-dimensional anatomical illustrations into three-dimensional computer images that could be rotated and viewed from any angle, for the benefit of students of medicine and biology. In 1988 this dream became the Visible Human Project™, under the sponsorship of the National Library of Medicine in Bethesda, Maryland. A grant was awarded to the University of Colorado School of Medicine, and in 1993 the first work of dissection and scanning began on the body of a Texas convict who had been executed by lethal injection. The process was repeated on the body of a Maryland woman who had died of a heart attack. Applying the latest techniques of computer graphics, the scientific team was able to create a series of three-dimensional digital images of the human body so beautiful and startlingly accurate that they seem more in the realm of art than science. On the computer screen, muscles, bones, and organs of the body can be turned and viewed from any angle, and layers of tissue can be electronically peeled away to reveal what lies underneath. In reproducing these digital images in two-dimensional print form, the editors at Rosen have tried to preserve the three-dimensional character of the work by showing organs of the body from different perspectives and using illustrations that progressively reveal deeper layers of anatomical structure.

Published in 2002 by The Rosen Publishing Group, Inc.
29 East 21st Street, New York, NY 10010

Copyright © 2002 by The Rosen Publishing Group, Inc.

All digital anatomy images copyright © 1999 by Visible Productions.

Digital anatomy images published by arrangement with Anatographica, LLC.
216 East 49th Street, New York, NY 10017

First Edition

Library of Congress Cataloging-in-Publication Data
Viegas, Jennifer
The eye: learning how we see / Jennifer Viegas.
p. cm. — (The 3-D library of the human body)
Includes bibliographical references and index.
Summary: Discusses the anatomy of the eye and how its sensory data are interpreted by the brain to give us vision.
ISBN 0-8239-3530-2
1. Vision—Juvenile literature. 2. Eye—Juvenile literature. [1.Vision. 2. Eye.]
I. Title. II. Series.
QP475.7 .V54 2001
612.8'4—dc21

2001004885

Manufactured in the United States of America

CONTENTS

PREFACE
COMPARATIVE
ANATOMY

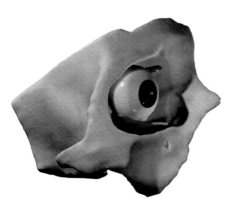

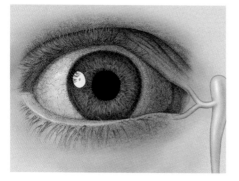

The founder of comparative anatomy, the science of comparing the anatomy of one species with the anatomy of another, was one of the giants of nineteenth-century science, George Leopold Chretien Frederic Dagobert, also known as Baron Cuvier (1769–1832). Cuvier originally planned to become a clergyman, but in 1795 a zoologist friend turned Cuvier's interest toward science and got him a position at the Museum of Natural History in Paris. From that point on, Cuvier began to establish a scientific reputation that almost nothing in the turbulent world of French politics or religion could destroy, though he was a Protestant in a predominantly Roman Catholic country, and he lived through the French Revolution and the Napoleonic Wars.

Cuvier studied the similarities and differences between the body parts of different animals as part of the great effort at classification of species that biologists were undertaking at the time. He became an expert in this field and was responsible for the division of the animal kingdom into four major groups, or phyla—vertebrata, mollusca, articulata, and radiata—based on the similarities of internal structures. But Cuvier also studied the relationship of body parts to their function and to an animal's lifestyle, and he discovered that some of these relationships were predictable. If, for example, he was shown the paw of an animal with sharp talons for catching prey, Cuvier could state with confidence that such an animal would also have sharp teeth for tearing flesh. It would also have a stomach adapted for digesting flesh, as well as other anatomical features of a predatory creature. Cuvier became so good at predicting these correlations it was said of him that from one look at a single bone he could reconstruct the entire animal. A famous story has one of his students bursting into his room in the middle of the night dressed up in a devil's costume shouting, "Cuvier, I have come to eat you!" Cuvier awoke, took one look, and replied, "All creatures with horns and hooves are herbivores. You can't eat me." Then he went back to sleep.

Cuvier also applied his comparative techniques to fossils. He demonstrated that the bones of a long-dead elephant were similar but not identical to those of the two living species of elephants. He identified the extinct creature *Megatherium* as a larger version of the modern ground sloth. It was Cuvier who gave the ancient flying reptile, the pterodactyl, its name. Yet, even though he was one of the first to perceive connections between ancient and modern organisms, Cuvier had a literal belief in the Bible's book of Genesis, and he totally rejected the theories of evolutionary biology that were circulating even before Darwin. Cuvier believed that fossils were the bones of animals killed in the great flood mentioned in Genesis, and that after the flood the Lord had simply recreated similar but new species of animals. He refused to accept the idea that these new species had descended from the ancient ones.

In spite of his refusal to accept any theory of evolution, Cuvier's work in comparing anatomical structures laid the foundation for the Darwinian theory that was to come approximately two decades after his death from cholera in 1832. The similarities and differences between the anatomies of ancient and modern species were evidence of the fact that organisms were changing over time, and it only remained for Charles Darwin to explain the mechanism of change: natural selection.

1
ANATOMY OF THE EYE

Thanks to sight, our perceived world has color, light, depth, and movement. Vision is possible because of the structure and inner workings of the eyes. Together with the brain, the eye allows us to experience the vibrant shades of a rainbow or the subtle shadows cast under a moonlit sky. Stand in front of a mirror or, with permission, look into the eyes of someone nearby. Notice what appears to be a black dot in the center of each eye. This black circle, called the pupil, is actually a hole that reveals the darkness of the inner eye. It is through this hole, and other parts of the eye, that light is able to enter from the outside world.

The Eye Socket

With your index finger, carefully touch the bony ridge underneath each eye. Following the contours of the bone, run your finger along its edges around the outside of the eye and toward the bridge of the nose. What you are feeling is the front section of the eye socket, sometimes referred to as the orbit. This bone extends into the head and is shaped like a small salad bowl. The scooped curve in the middle helps to hold the eyeball in place.

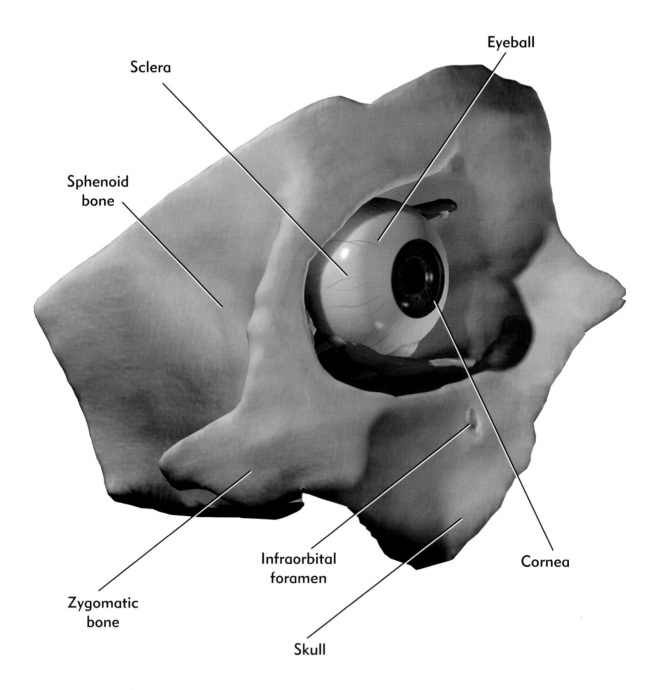

Eyeball

Sclera

Sphenoid
bone

Zygomatic
bone

Infraorbital
foramen

Skull

Cornea

This illustration shows the position of the right eye and eye socket within the facial bones. The eye socket is set deep within the skull to offer protection to the eyeball.

As the word "eyeball" suggests, each eye is a round ball with an almost invisible bump at the front, the cornea. On average, eyeballs measure one inch in diameter. Muscles connected to the eyeball within the socket allow the eyes to swivel.

The Conjunctiva

The front of each eye appears to be shiny and smooth, almost like a thin layer of glass. That is because the eyes are covered with a transparent layer called the conjunctiva. The conjunctiva is a mucous membrane, or a thin, pliable section of tissue. The semiliquid mucous it secretes lubricates each eye, and, like window-washer fluid, helps to keep the eyes clean.

The Cornea

The cornea serves as our window to the world. Like a window, the cornea is transparent so that light can travel through it. The cornea is shaped like a curved disk and is located at the front of the eye. It is able to focus on objects and gather visual information about them.

Seventy-five percent of the eye's power rests in the cornea, yet it is extremely small. At its center, each cornea is only about half a millimeter thick. At its sides near the sclera—the tough white part of the eye—each cornea becomes slightly thicker, but only by about another one-half millimeter.

Despite its very small size, each cornea consists of five different layers of tissue. The first layer, closest to the conjunctiva and the outside of the eye, is called the epithelium. It is like a very thin, clear sheet of skin. Next comes the Bowman's layer. It is made of sturdy, elastic material that gives the cornea flexibility. Underneath the Bowman's layer is the stromal layer. This is the thickest section of the

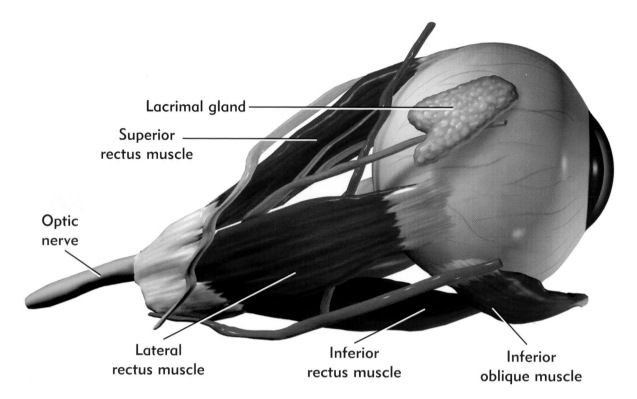

This lateral (side) view of the right eye reveals its muscles and the optic nerve that conveys impulses from the eye to the brain.

cornea. It consists of collagen, which is a tough, fibrous tissue also found in skin and bones. This layer contains antigens that produce antibodies. They help to keep the eyes free from infection.

The fourth layer of the cornea is called the endothelium. Unlike the stroma, the endothelium is quite thin, with the thickness of only one cell. It is extremely fragile and, once damaged, cannot heal itself. That is one reason why we have protective eyelids. The endothelium helps to maintain water pressure in the eye and promotes transparency. The fifth and final layer is called the Descemet's membrane. It consists of a thin sheet of elastic tissue that, like the Bowman's layer, provides a certain amount of movement and flexibility to the cornea.

The Aqueous Humor

In anatomy the word "humor" refers to bodily fluids. In this case, the aqueous humor is the fluid located behind the cornea. The chemical composition of the aqueous humor is somewhat like blood, but it does not have blood's high protein content. However, the fluid does contain nutrients, such as sugars and amino acids, to enrich the cornea and the front section of the eye. Such nutrition is essential, because the cornea itself does not have blood vessels. If it did, the cornea would lose its transparency.

The aqueous humor has two other important functions. It helps to keep the eye firm. By moving continuously, it also distributes nutrients and removes waste materials. The waste drains out through the

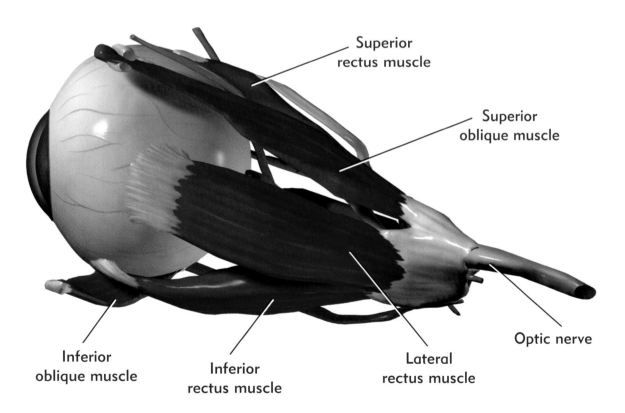

Another view of the right eye shows the muscles that control the movement of the eyeball.

What Determines Eye Color

Irises give each of us a unique eye color. Some people have brown eyes, while others may have blue or green eyes. The color is inherited from our parents. Interestingly enough, only one pigment creates different color variations—melanin.

Melanin is the substance that gives skin, hair, and the irises a brown coloring. People with brown eyes have a lot of melanin, and usually have darker skin and hair. Blue-eyed individuals, on the other hand, possess little melanin and often have lighter skin and hair. Green-eyed people have slightly more melanin, but still tend to have lighter-toned skin and hair.

canal of Schlemm, a channel that circles around the cornea. Tears perform a similar function. With each blink, the lacrimal glands above the upper eyelids wash antibacterial tears over the eyes to protect and clean them. Tears leave the eyes through ducts that drain through the nose. That is why you sometimes have to blow your nose after crying.

The Iris and Pupil

Behind the aqueous humor are the iris and pupil. As previously mentioned, the pupil is just a hole. The iris, the colored portion of the eye, determines how large this hole should be. Like strings opening a curtain on a stage, ciliary muscles pull the iris open and shut. When it is dark, the iris opens wide to permit more light to enter the eye. In bright sunlight, the iris closes up to protect the eye from too much light.

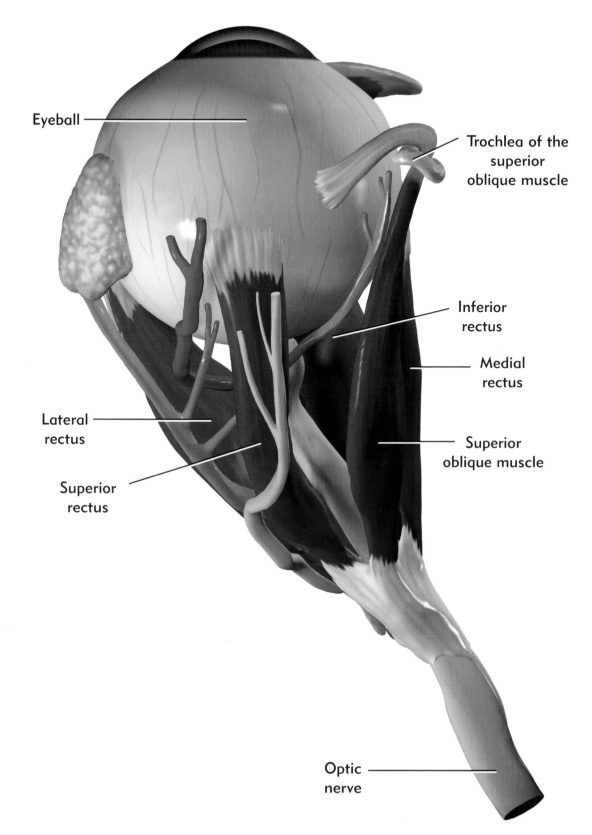

Eyeball

Trochlea of the superior oblique muscle

Inferior rectus

Medial rectus

Lateral rectus

Superior oblique muscle

Superior rectus

Optic nerve

This superior (top) view of the eye shows the extrinsic muscles and the optic nerve.

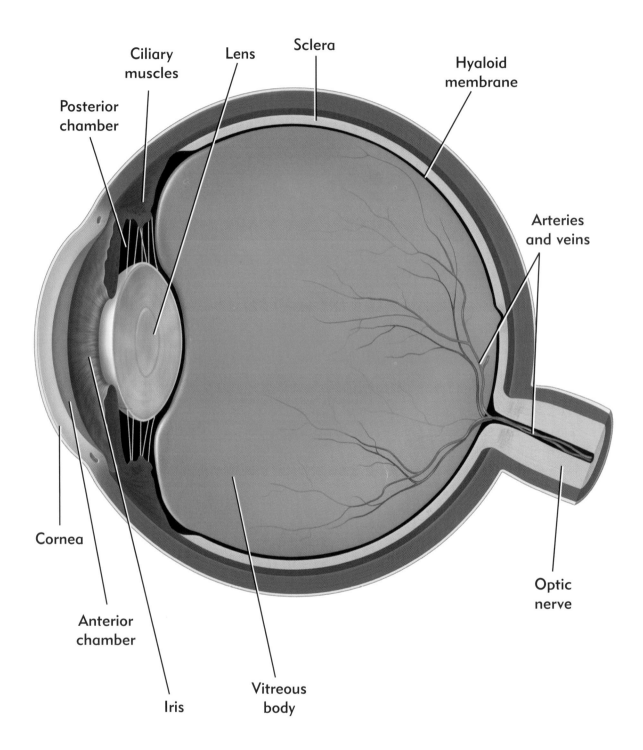

Ciliary
muscles

Lens

Sclera

Hyaloid
membrane

Posterior
chamber

Arteries
and veins

Cornea

Optic
nerve

Anterior
chamber

Iris

Vitreous
body

This cross-sectional view of the interior of the eyeball reveals the parts
that enable us to see.

The Lens

Directly behind each pupil is the lens. Looking somewhat like a contact lens, this part of the eye can change shape to focus the light entering the eye, a process begun by the cornea. Stringlike ciliary muscles are attached to the top and bottom of the lens. When the muscles pull, the lens becomes more flat and narrow. This happens when we look at faraway objects.

Behind the lens is a substance known as the vitreous humor. It is a thick, white fluid that gives the eyes their firm, rubbery texture. Vitreous humor fills up most of the central chamber of each eye.

The Retina

The inside of the eyeball, behind the vitreous humor, is lined with light-sensitive layers of cells. They form the retina, which serves as the film in the eye's camera. The retina contains two types of cells: rods and cones. Amazingly, each retina has 150 rods and 10 million cones.

Rods do not perceive color, but they work well in low-light conditions. They are good at defining clear, sharp images. Cones do just the opposite. They detect color but provide little clarity when light is low. Most of the rods and cones are centered in an area of the retina at the inside back of the eye called the fovea, or macula.

THE EYE-BRAIN CONNECTION

Just as film from a camera must be removed for development, images captured on the retina have to leave the eyes so that the pictures may be fully processed. What makes human sight better than even the most high-tech cameras is that the processing occurs in a split second, with most images simultaneously filed away for future reference in our memories. The eyes function like a camera while the brain handles all image development and processing. Nerves connect the eyes to the brain.

The Optic Nerve

Nerves are bundles of special tissue that carry messages to and from the brain. Through chemical changes that create electrical impulses, nerves throughout the body can control everything from movement to sight. In a chain reaction, individual nerve cells, called neurons, pass electrical impulses to each other until the contained message reaches its destination. Like the plastic coating surrounding an electrical cord, a material called myelin forms a protective sheath around each nerve cell.

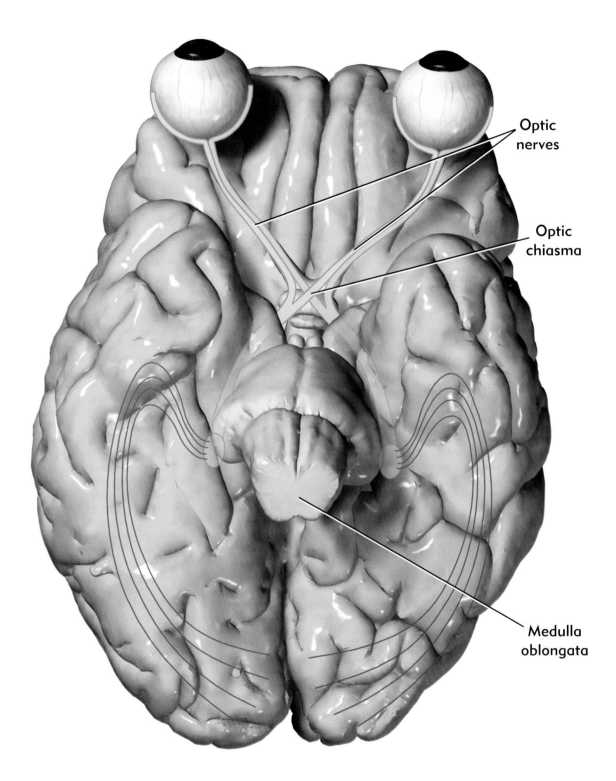

Optic nerves

Optic chiasma

Medulla oblongata

This view of the brain from underneath shows how the two optic nerves cross over each other to opposite sides of the brain.

The Blind Spot

The place where the optic nerve meets the back of the eye creates a natural blind spot because this area does not contain any light-sensing rods or cones. Since the eyes and brain usually compensate for the blocked view, we do not notice that anything is missing.

You can, however, find the blind spot for one eye by drawing two inch-high letters or shapes three inches apart on a straight line. Close your right eye and focus your left eye on the left object, holding the piece of paper at arm's length. Now, slowly bring the paper close to your face. The right object seems to disappear!

Tiny nerve fibers are connected to each of the retina's millions of rod and cone cells. These cells begin the chain reaction process by collecting information about objects, such as their size, shape, and color. The information in the cells transfers to the nerve fibers, which come together toward the back of the eye until they form the optic nerve.

This connection is similar to the electrical wires found at the back of most computer systems. Small wires join the basic components, while a larger cable connects the entire system to an outlet. The optic nerve functions like the computer's main cable. It gathers all of the nerve fibers from the retinas into two easy-to-manage bundles.

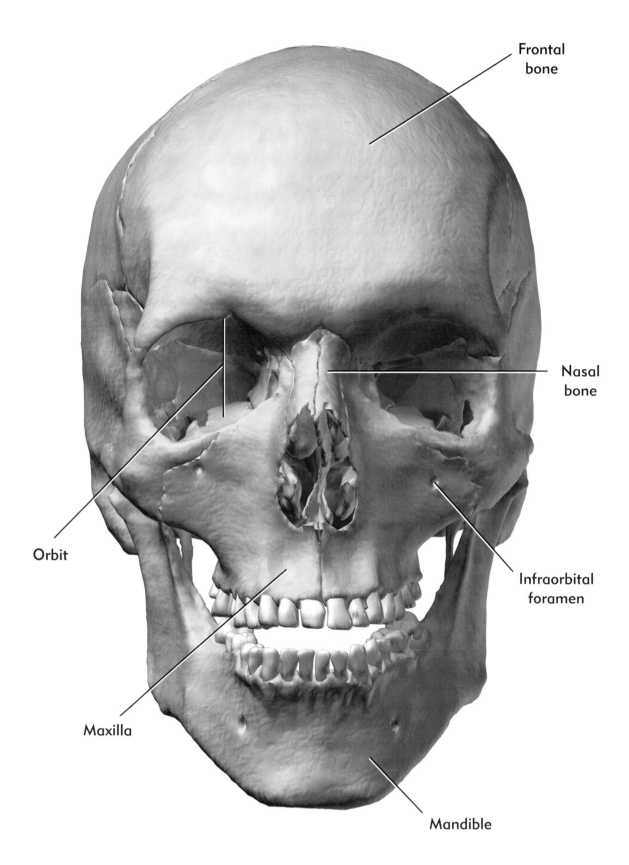

Frontal
bone

Nasal
bone

Infraorbital
foramen

Orbit

Maxilla

Mandible

An anterior (front) view of the skull. The eye sockets are in the middle of the head and are surrounded by a protective layer of bone.

The Blood Supply to the Eyes and Optic Nerves

A layer in the eye just above the retina, called the choroid, helps to maintain and feed the retina. Nutrients and oxygen are able to reach the retina through a network of blood vessels in the choroid. Arteries bring in nourishment, while veins carry out waste products.

Just as small nerve fibers gather to form the optic nerve, the arteries and veins merge into larger blood vessels that serve the optic nerve. The main artery that delivers blood to the optic nerve is called the central retinal artery. It runs down the middle of the entire optic nerve. The central retinal vein corresponds to this artery and helps to drain waste material and fluid out of the retina.

The Optic Chiasma

Place a hand over your right eye. Pay attention to what your left eye can see. Now place a hand over your left eye and make a mental note of what is visible. As you probably noticed, each eye has a slightly different view. Yet despite these two differing views, we have just one field of vision. This is made possible, in part, because of the transfer of information that takes place at the optic chiasma.

Optic nerves running from the left and right eyes merge at the optic chiasma in the brain, near the pituitary gland. Here, some of the data collected by rods and cones in the right eye is mixed with information collected by the rods and cones in the left eye.

Lateral Geniculate Body

After the optic chiasma crossover, the two optic nerves fan out again in the brain. They then curve inward and meet at a place called the lateral geniculate body. It looks like two small balloons stuck together on top of three tiny eggs. As at the optic chiasma, the optic nerves exchange information at the lateral geniculate body. There the brain analyzes how the two pupils react to observed light levels.

Optic Radiation

After leaving the lateral geniculate body, the optic nerves fan out again, forming a heart shape around the parts of the brain called the temporal lobes. The temporal lobes handle hearing and smell, so the optic nerves take a detour around this section. The heart-shaped path that they take is called the optic radiation because "radiate" means to spread out.

Internal Capsule

Near the bottom of the heart shape where the two optic nerves meet is the internal capsule. It is the last point of exchange before information collected by the optic nerves heads into the final processing stage in the brain. The internal capsule houses most of the body's data concerning movement and the senses. Here, other nerves pick up information about spatial awareness and memory from the optic nerves. This data is sent to the prefrontal lobes, which are areas in the brain that specialize in depth perception and memory.

Primary and Secondary Visual Cortices

The nerve signals traveling along the optic nerve finish their journey at the back of the brain in the area of the visual cortices. The primary visual cortex is located at the very back of the brain and head. The secondary visual cortex is directly in front of it. To get an idea of where these are located, take a hand and run it up the back of your neck and across the back of the head. Where the skull slightly bulges out is approximately where the visual cortices are, about an inch away from your fingers under the skull bone and a layer of fluid.

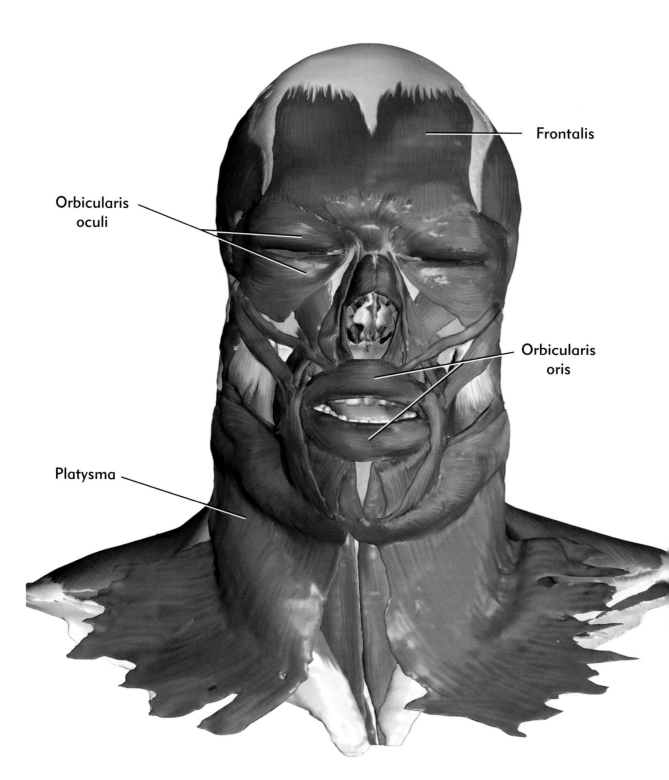

Frontalis

Orbicularis
oculi

Orbicularis
oris

Platysma

The muscles of the face are shown here. The orbicularis oculi control the
opening and closing of the eyelids.

22

The visual cortices break down the information collected from the eyes into separate components, such as what colors, motion, and shapes are being observed. The secondary visual cortex then processes all of the data and identifies the objects in the field of vision, drawing upon prior memories and experiences.

For example, let's say you see someone who looks familiar to you across a crowded room, but you cannot quite place his or her face. Your eyes first spot the person and collect information about what he or she looks like. This information travels through the brain and ends up at the visual cortices. The secondary visual cortex compares the data with information already stored in your brain's memory. Sometimes when a match is made it feels like a lightbulb is going off in your head. It is that moment when you finally remember who the person is.

Every waking moment, millions of nerve signals shoot through the brain and continually provide information about the people and the world around us. An almost magical feature of the visual cortices is that they allow us not only to see images in real time, but, because they store data to memory, they also enable us to recreate images, shapes, and colors in our imaginations. This way, we can create mental images of things we have viewed in the past. For example, when a friend or relative is away and you miss him or her, you can remember what the individual looks like because data about the person is stored in your brain.

3
VISION

Light is the medium by which information concerning the world around us is transmitted to the eyes. This sounds complicated, but really the concept is very simple. At some point, you have probably been in a room or a closet that was so dark you could not see a thing. The objects in the room were still present even though they were not visible to you. If a flashlight had been turned on, only the areas near where the light shined would have been visible. That is because eyes pick up information based on the way light bounces off of objects.

By itself, light travels in a straight line. But when light passes through certain materials, it can reflect and bend. In a dark room, try shining a flashlight in a mirror set at a right angle to a wall, such as a bathroom mirror. What do you see on the wall? The circle of light reflects onto the wall from the mirror, even though the light did not initially travel in that direction.

Because of their glasslike transparency and structure, the cornea and lens of the eye can bend light. Camera lenses have this ability, too, but often the lens has to be manually adjusted or changed to match the position of the object in the field of vision. The human eyes and muscles make such adjustments by themselves.

How Eyes See Objects

Let's examine how, at this very second, your eyes are creating a visual image of this book. First, light reflected from the book hits the cornea. At this point the light entering your eye has already been condensed into manageable rays. Because light condenses information about objects and is able to bend, you can see the book even though it is much larger than your eyes. Televisions operate using a similar process.

Light bends when it hits the cornea and travels toward the iris. Ciliary muscles around the iris react to light in the room and cause the iris to open or close around the pupil. The muscles can cause

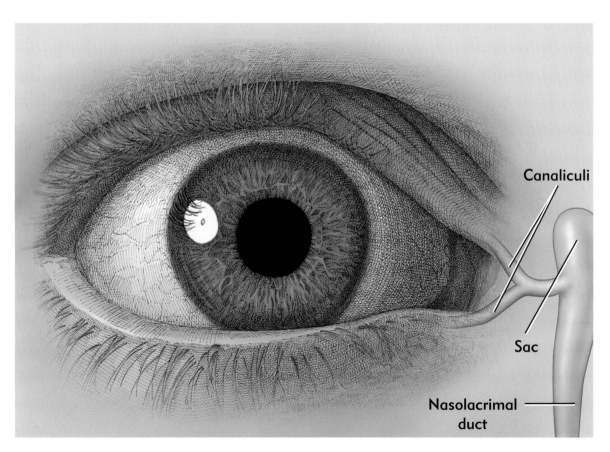

This illustration reveals the connection between the tear ducts and the eye.

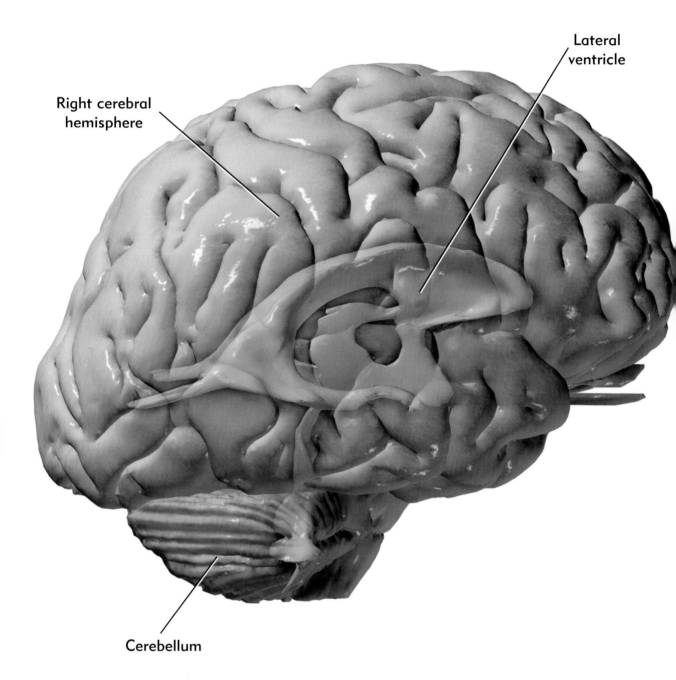

Right cerebral
hemisphere

Lateral
ventricle

Cerebellum

Signals from the eyes travel through the optic nerve to the back of the brain, where the images are recreated and interpreted in a process that is still largely unexplained.

the pupil to open anywhere from 1/25 of an inch—if light conditions are extremely bright—to 1/3 of an inch under darker conditions. Light travels through the pupil hole, where it reaches the lens.

Since it is likely that this book is close to your face, the lens identifies the book as a near object and the eye adjusts its focus accordingly. For near objects, eye muscles contract to make the lens short and round. If the book were far away, the eye muscles would cause the lens to become thin and long. These different shapes change the way the lens bends light. After passing through the lens, the light that initially bounced off the book reaches the light-sensing rod and cone cells on the retina at the back of the eye. Like a movie projector, the lens projects an image of the book on the retina. Surprisingly, the image is upside down!

Optical Illusions

Optical illusions are visual tricks that fool the brain. Since the brain must process information collected in the eyes, it learns to react to certain patterns. When these patterns are broken, the brain still functions as it normally would and an optical illusion may result.

Try this trick. Roll a sheet of paper into a tube. Hold the tube up to your right eye with your right hand while holding your left hand, palm facing forward, at the side end of the tube. Gradually bring your left hand toward your face, running it alongside the tube. The brain registers that you have a hole in your left hand!

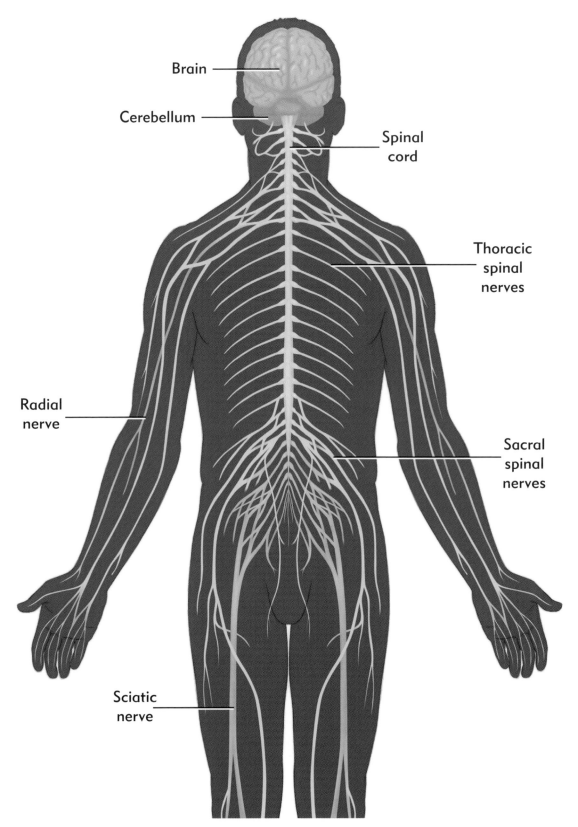

Brain

Cerebellum

Spinal cord

Thoracic spinal nerves

Radial nerve

Sacral spinal nerves

Sciatic nerve

The nerves branch out from the spinal cord to all areas of the body. Eye-muscle coordination is controlled by the nervous system, and the nerves ensure that we respond properly to what we see.

This inverted image is what the optic nerve carries with it as nerve impulses send the image of the book to the brain's optic chiasma, the lateral geniculate body, the optic radiation, the internal capsule, and finally to the primary and secondary visual cortices. The book does not appear to be upside down because the brain transposes the image to match what the brain thinks it should be seeing. Humans are not born with this skill. It has to be learned. Newborn babies, for example, can see, but they have no sense of direction. Over a short period of time they learn to associate the position of objects in relation to other things, and soon see right-side-up.

After the brain has finished processing the now right-side-up object in the visual cortex region, the mind creates an instantaneous mental image of the book and stores this image away in memory. Since memory can last for many years, the image of this book, and the information gleaned from it, may last in your memory well into the future.

Stereoscopic Vision

If we had one big eye in the middle of our foreheads it would not only look rather odd, but we would also not have very good depth perception, or the ability to gauge the distance from one object to another. Two eyes allow us to see everything in 3-D, or three dimensions. This ability is called stereoscopic vision.

Stereoscopic vision is possible because each eye has a slightly different field of vision. The brain combines the two images into one when the two optic nerves leading from each eye send impulses down the nerve pathways toward the visual cortex region. While the images captured in the left and right eyes are combined and processed by the brain, we still retain information about what was seen by each individual eye.

Contact Lenses

Unlike eyeglasses, which are worn on the face, contact lenses are inserted directly over the cornea. This has certain advantages and disadvantages. On the plus side, contacts provide good peripheral, or side, vision. They stay in place during high impact activities, such as sports, and they provide a nearly invisible way to correct nearsightedness, farsightedness, and astigmatism.

Contacts, however, require more maintenance than do eyeglasses, and must be kept clean at all times. Some people also find them uncomfortable to wear. If you need corrective lenses, your optometrist should provide advice and information about obtaining either eyeglasses or contacts.

In sports, sometimes people will try to improve their ability to judge distance. Many golfers, for example, will try to determine a ball's distance and direction from the hole by squatting on the ground to provide a more level field of vision, or by closing one eye to devote their attention to a single area. Target shooters, pool players, and darts players will also often close one eye to improve direct focus on a single target and to eliminate some of the 3-D effects of stereoscopic vision.

Seeing Colors

Cone cells in the retina allow humans to detect three basic colors in light: red, green, and blue. Each of these three colors stimulates a slightly different type of cone cell. Variations in the intensity of these colors and the processing performed by the brain give us the ability to detect a full rainbow spectrum of colors.

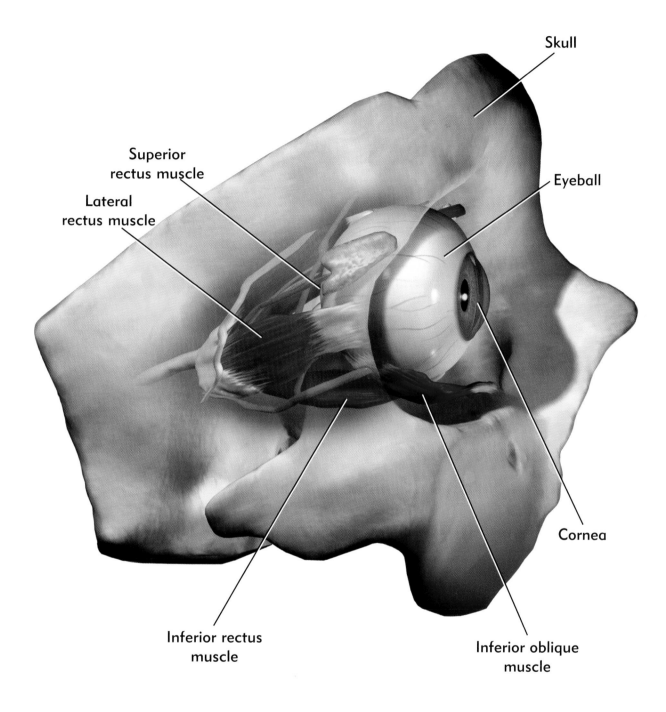

Skull

Superior
rectus muscle

Lateral
rectus muscle

Eyeball

Cornea

Inferior rectus
muscle

Inferior oblique
muscle

This view of the right eyeball within its socket shows the muscles that move the eye.

Each cone cell contains 100 million molecules of a substance called a photopigment. These retinal molecules chemically change in the presence of light because all light contains a certain amount of energy. For example, think of how light from the sun can produce solar energy. When struck by light, a retinal molecule twists around, which causes other chemical reactions to take place inside the cone. The cone then generates a nerve impulse that travels through the optic nerve to the brain, which registers the observed color. Incredibly, this multistep process occurs many millions of times each second in each of the eye's cone cells.

Sometimes, colors in bright light can leave a lasting image on the retina. You may have experienced this after having your picture taken with a camera that uses a flash. When this happens, the round light of the flash remains in your field of vision for a few seconds after the picture was snapped. The light-sensing cells of the retina become overstimulated. Staring at direct sunlight and other bright objects can also overstimulate cells in the eye and may cause permanent damage.

4

VISION DISORDERS

Good vision requires that all of the various parts and systems involved in sight are working properly. Optometrists, or eye doctors, check to make sure that the cornea and lens focus correctly. They check the eyes' sensitivity to different light levels. They also measure the pressure of the fluid within the eyeballs.

Eye charts allow optometrists to determine how well you can see both up close and at a distance. Letters or numbers on the chart usually begin large and get smaller and smaller. Individuals who can see clearly at the prescribed distance of twenty feet, and who do not experience eyestrain, are said to have 20/20 vision, or normal eyesight.

Just as with a car or computer with many sophisticated parts, problems can affect one or more of the parts of the body involved in sight. Sometimes these problems come at birth, with structural faults in the eyeball or lens. Age is also a factor. Just as a car or computer can develop problems over time, so too can the eyes. Certain parts simply wear out and need to be treated or replaced. By far the most common visual defects are nearsightedness and farsightedness, with up to 60 percent of people having these conditions.

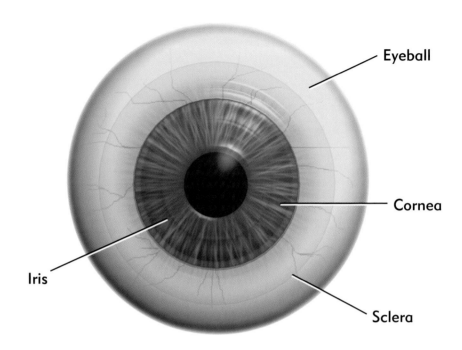

Eyeball

Cornea

Iris

Sclera

The eye holds an irresistible fascination for us. It has been called the window to the soul.

Nearsightedness

Nearsightedness, or myopia, occurs when a person has long eyeballs or lenses that refract too much. Refraction refers to the bending of light. Nearsighted individuals can see objects that are close to them but have trouble distinguishing objects that are far away. For example, a nearsighted person standing in front of a classroom or an auditorium may be able to see clearly the first few rows of people, but the rest of the room looks like a fuzzy blur.

Good vision requires that the focal point, or the place where light waves converge in the eye, hits the retina. The light rays enter the eye in a V shape, with the open part of the V corresponding to the top and bottom of an object. In a person with 20/20 vision, the pointy V convergence usually lands right on the fovea, where most of the eye's rod and cone cells are located. In a person with near-sightedness, the convergence, or the point of perfect focus, occurs in front of the retina.

Nearsightedness is easily cleared up with corrective lenses, meaning either eyeglasses or contact lenses. The corrective lens for myopia is concave, or hollow and curved inward, like the inside of a bowl. The concave lens extends the light wave convergence in the eye to the retina.

Farsightedness

Farsightedness, or hyperopia, allows affected individuals to view objects clearly that are far away, but nearby objects appear blurred. Weak lenses that cannot produce enough refraction or eyeballs that are too short in shape are the causes of farsightedness. The eyeball of a farsighted person looks a bit like an egg standing upright. The eyeball of a nearsighted person looks more like an egg resting on its side.

Light convergence in the eyes of a farsighted person falls past the retina. The pointy end of the V goes past the eye. Wearing convex corrective lenses can solve this problem. Convex means to curve outward. The disklike shape allows the individual to focus light rays onto the retina.

Astigmatism

Another eye problem that can be corrected by wearing either eye-glasses or contact lenses is called astigmatism. A person with this condition may have an irregularly curved cornea or an irregularity in the shape of the eyeball. With astigmatism, rays of light entering the eye bend in different ways. Some are focused correctly, while others may bend too much. This causes distortion of viewed objects. For example, the person may see a slightly blurry double image of an object that otherwise appears clear. With this condition, objects viewed at all distances can be affected.

Astigmatism is corrected by wearing cylindrical lenses, which look a bit like tubes that have been sliced in half. This shape helps to bend light inward to create a proper focus of light convergence on the retina.

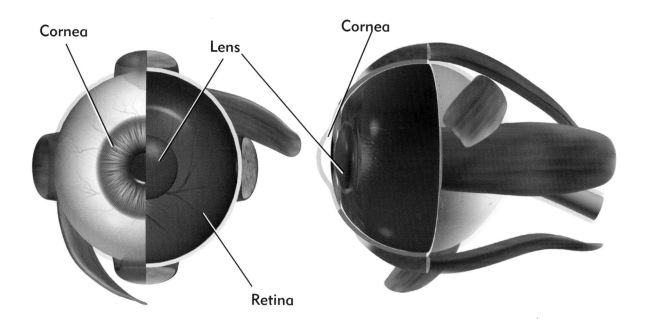

Cornea

Lens

Cornea

Retina

These anterior (front) and lateral (side) views of the eyeball have parts cut away to reveal the lens and the surface of the retina.

Colorblindness

Though rare in females, approximately 8 percent of males inherit a condition known as colorblindness. People with this condition are missing one or more types of cones for a certain color group. Red-green color blindness is most common and prevents the person from distinguishing between red and green. Usually the problem is not very serious, because most shades of red are not pure and have a bit of yellow in them, and most greens contain some blue. Therefore, colorblind people who drive generally do not have difficulties seeing changing traffic lights.

Glaucoma

Other more serious diseases can affect the eye and may cause permanent damage. Glaucoma, for example, is a disease that disrupts the flow of the aqueous humor in front of the iris and pupil. The change in flow may then cause pressure to build in the entire eye. That is why eye doctors usually measure your eye pressure.

If the disease is identified early, medication or surgery can restore proper aqueous humor flow. If the disease is left untreated, the high pressure can destroy cells in the retina and cause vision loss or blindness. Certain individuals can be predisposed to developing glaucoma because of genetic factors or complications from diabetes or high blood pressure.

Cataracts

Over time, cells in the lens of the eye can lose their transparency and cloud up, like a window covered with a white film. The cloudy, opaque areas are called cataracts. Although the condition is painless, it can cause blurred vision and difficulty in distinguishing colors.

Surgery usually corrects the problem. Doctors can remove the affected lens and can either replace it with a new one or restore the lost vision with corrective lenses.

Macular Degeneration

As the human life span continues to increase, so too does the risk of developing macular degeneration. When a person gets older, blood flow to the eye may decrease, causing a lack of oxygen and nutrients in the retina. Rods and cones in the macula, or fovea, are especially sensitive to such changes and can gradually deteriorate, causing loss of vision.

Blindness

Blindness, or complete vision loss, can occur at birth or as a result of an illness or an accident. The damage or defect may be in the eyes or in the brain region. But because the brain is involved in the vision process and is highly adaptable, blind individuals can compensate for the loss of vision with other senses, such as hearing and touch. Many blind people, for example, read using a special raised alphabet known as Braille. Patterns of dots coinciding with letters can be felt with the fingertips. Guide dogs can also help blind individuals to lead more independent lives. The dogs are trained to be the eyes of the owners, thus enabling people to navigate safely outdoors and in unfamiliar places.

GLOSSARY

aqueous humor   Fluid located between the cornea and lens that nourishes and protects the eye. It also helps to maintain proper pressure within the eyeball.

astigmatism   Condition caused by an irregularly curved cornea or an irregularity in the shape of the eyeball. Astigmatism distorts images, making them seem blurry or doubled.

blind spot   The place where the optic nerve leaves the eye. Because this small region of the eye does not contain any rods or cones, it creates a blind area in our fields of vision. Since the brain makes up for the missing view, we do not usually notice the blind spot.

ciliary muscles   Small, stringlike muscles that change the shape of the lens and help to open and close the iris.

cones   Light-sensing cells within the retina that allow us to see color.

conjunctiva   Transparent, protective outer first layer of the eye.

cornea   Clear, five-layered disk at the front of the eye that helps with focusing. It does 75 percent of the eye's work.

corrective lenses Eyeglasses or contact lenses that can correct eye problems, such as astigmatism, nearsightedness, and farsightedness, by changing the way that the eye bends and focuses light.

farsightedness A condition, commonly caused by eyeballs that are too short or lenses that are too weak, that keeps affected individuals from clearly seeing nearby objects. They can, however, see objects at a distance.

fovea Also called the macula, the fovea is the part of the retina containing the most rod and cone cells. Light that converges here produces the clearest images.

iris This colored part of the eye controls how much light can enter through the pupil.

lens Transparent, flexible disk located behind the pupil that focuses light, a process begun by the cornea.

melanin Substance that gives color to the iris, skin, and hair.

nearsightedness A condition, commonly caused by eyeballs that are too long or lenses that refract too much, that prohibits affected individuals from clearly seeing objects that are far away.

optic chiasma Place in the brain where the optic nerves from each eye meet to exchange information.

optic nerve Nerve that runs from the retina of each eye. It carries information from the eye's light-sensing cells through the brain.

pupil   Hole through which light enters the eye.

refraction   The bending of light.

retina   Lining the back of the eye, the retina contains light-sensing cells that enable us to interpret images from light reflected off of objects.

rods   Named for their shape, rods are light-sensing cells in the retina that define clear, sharp images, even in low light.

sclera   Tough white part of the eye.

tears   Protective fluid, made in the lacrimal glands just above the eyes and released through the inside of the upper eyelids, that helps to protect the eyes from dust, germs, and other things that could cause damage.

20/20 vision   Term used to describe individuals with normal vision who can, without eyestrain, clearly see at the prescribed distance of twenty feet.

visual cortex   The rear portion of the brain that processes visual information supplied by the optic nerve.

vitreous humor   Thick, jelly-like fluid located in the main chamber of each eye, behind the lens, that gives the eyes their rubbery texture.

FOR MORE INFORMATION

Web Sites

The American Optometric Association

http://www.aoanet.org

The AOA's online educational center provides information on optical illusions, how the eye works, and more. The site also includes sections for both teachers and students.

Magazines

Scientific American Explorations

415 Madison Avenue

New York, NY 10017

(212) 451-8300

This publication for young adults covers science and technology.

Interactive and Multimedia CD-ROMs

The Human 3D CD-ROM

by Mega Systems

Multimedia featuring three-dimensional views of the human body.

Interactive Human Body CD-ROM

by Mega Systems

Viewers can zoom in on any part of the body to learn about anatomy.

Our Body CD-ROM

by Mega Systems

Multimedia that educates users about the human body.

FOR FURTHER READING

Ardley, Neil. *Science Book of the Senses*. San Diego, CA: Harcourt Brace, 1992.

Byles, Monica. *Experiment with Senses*. Minneapolis, MN: Lerner Publishing Group, 1993.

Dispenzio, Michael. *Eye-Popping Optical Illusions*. New York: Sterling Publishing Company, 2001.

Farndon, John. *The Big Book of the Brain: All About the Body's Control Center*. New York: Peter Bedrick Books, 2000.

Heian International Publishing Incorporated, eds. *All About Our Bodies: Our Eyes, Ears and Noses*. Torrance, CA: Heian International Publishing Incorporated, 1996.

Llamas, Andreu. *Sight* (The Five Senses of the Animal World). New York: Chelsea House Publishers, 1996.

Nurosi, Aki. *Colorful Illusions: Tricks to Fool Your Eyes*. New York: Sterling Publishing Company, 2000.

Parker, Steve. *Eyewitness: The Human Body.* New York: Dorling Kindersley Publishing, Inc., 1999.

Ripoll, Jaime. *How Our Senses Work* (The Invisible World). New York: Chelsea House Publishers, 1994.

Silverstein, Alvin. *Can You See the Chalkboard?* (My Health). New York: Franklin Watts, Inc., 2001.

INDEX

About the Author

Jennifer Viegas, a nearsighted writer with contacts and several cool pairs of glasses, is a reporter for *Discovery News* and is a features columnist for Knight Ridder Newspapers. She has worked as a journalist for ABC News, PBS, *The Washington Post*, *The Christian Science Monitor*, and several other publications.

Photo Credits

Cover, pp. 1, 4 (middle and bottom), 8, 10, 11, 13, 14, 17, 19, 22, 25, 26, 28, 31 © Visible Productions, by arrangement with Anatographica, LLC; pp. 4 (top), 34, 36 © Williams & Wilkins, a Waverly Company.

Series Design

Claudia Carlson

Layout

Tahara Hasan